Racism

Deal with it
before it
gets under
your skin

Anne Marie Aikins • Illustrated by Steven Murray

James Lorimer & Company Ltd., Publishers
Toronto

Some kids from

the neighborhood are all set to play a pick-up game of basketball. The team captains are choosing their players.

It's just like any other Saturday afternoon, but this time you notice something: all the Black kids are being scooped up first, including the ones who aren't especially athletic.

And even though some of the Asian kids, like yourself, are really fast and have all the moves, you keep being passed over. What's going on here?

You've just experienced racism.

Racism starts with the belief that people can be divided into groups called races. These groupings are based on physical traits, such as skin colour. Racism is the idea that some races are superior to others and should have more power than others. It is a form of prejudice — or pre-judging a person based on the group they belong to.

Everyone deserves to be accepted as the person they are, not just as a member of a certain group.

This book will help you understand that there really is only one race — the human race — and we're all part of it. If you have ever felt hurt by racism (lots of people have), this book will help you protect yourself. If you've ever had a racist thought (most of us have), this book will help you recognize your prejudices.

We have all witnessed racism in one form or another. Read on to find out how to identify it, avoid it, and deal with it.

Contents

What is

So thinking an Asian person won't be good at basketball is racist, right? Sure, but what about when we assume that same person will be good at math? Well, those ideas about Asians are both stereotypes. A stereotype is when you have a set image of what a person from a certain group will be like. You see, stereotypes are usually negative, but not always. That's why so many people don't even recognize them. Have you ever seen racial stereotypes in action?

What about:

- assuming a person is rich?

- assuming someone can't afford to pay?

- making someone feel excluded?

- always choosing kids from certain groups to be leaders?

- assuming someone will have a special talent?

- assuming someone is less intelligent or educated?

- spreading gossip about a certain group?

- name-calling?

racism?

- being dismissive of someone's celebrations?

- blaming someone for other people's problems?

- labeling someone as a drug-user or alcoholic?

- making fun of someone's appearance or clothing?

- suspecting someone is going to break a rule or shoplift?

Stereotypes can lead to prejudice. And these attitudes can lead to discrimination, or treating people differently because of the group they belong to. Racism is discrimination that is based on race. To put it a different way, racism occurs when someone has the power to act on his or her racist attittudes.

Racism 101

BLAMES

IT'S HAILLE'S FIRST DAY AT SCHOOL IN CANADA.

Class, this is Haille. He just arrived in Canada.

It's *always* unfair when

LABELS

COREEN'S CLASS IS READING ABOUT FIRST NATIONS PEOPLE.

THEY FIND OUT THAT COREEN IS FROM THE MOHAWK NATION.

My grandfather is a chief.

EXCLUDES

DAVID IS JEWISH

AND OFTEN SKIPS THE CHRISTMAS CELEBRATIONS AT SCHOOL .

No problem.

THE STUDENT COUNCIL DECIDES ON THE DATE FOR THE ANNUAL DANCE.

What about this day?

We can't have it during Christmas break.

ASSUMES

PAT IS SURPRISED WHEN THE NEW KID ASKS TO BE HIS LAB PARTNER

HE LIES AND SAYS THAT SOMEONE ELSE ALREADY ASKED HIM.

Whaddya say? Partners?

Sorry.

Psst!

Dad says immigrants are taking all the good jobs.

HAILLE FEELS EMBARRASSED AND CONFUSED.

HE FAKES BEING SICK SO HE DOESN'T HAVE TO GO TO SCHOOL.

Ugh!

meone . . .

THEY THINK THEY KNOW WHAT REAL FIRST NATIONS PEOPLE ARE LIKE FROM THE MEDIA.

Does she live on a reserve?

She must be poor.

Don't people on reserves do drugs?

THEY WONDER IF THAT MAKES COREEN REALLY DIFFERENT FROM THEM.

Why don't they just ask me?

THE DANCE IS SCHEDULED FOR THE FIRST DAY OF HANUKKAH.

8 DANCE 9
Hanukkah
15 16

DAVID IS DISAPPOINTED AT BEING LEFT OUT ONCE MORE.

WINTER DANCE! Dec.8

Hanukkah is on every calendar, for Pete's sake.

PAT TALKS TO HIS FRIENDS ABOUT IT.

I wonder what that skinhead is up to?

THE NEW KID WONDERS WHAT HE DID WRONG...

None of the cool kids will hang with me.

AND BOTH KIDS LOSE OUT.

QUIZ

Having trouble figuring out whether you're dealing with racism or something else? Remember, when your belief in racial stereotypes harms others or puts them at a disadvantage — even unintentionally — that's racism. You decide whether each of the following situations is an example of racism. Check out your answers on the following page.

1 Asian Frustration

Kenny called a kid at school Chinese, but now he thinks she might be Korean or maybe Vietnamese.

2 THE OUTSIDER

Jenny notices she is always the last one to be picked for games by the other girls.

3 Just a Joke

Mike tells a "Newfie" joke, and makes everyone laugh.

4 NOT PLAYING BY THE NUMBERS

Lien's teacher gives her a B- in math, saying he expected more from someone with her background.

5 FRIENDLY FIRE

Jamal and Peter get into an argument in the schoolyard and call each other names, like "jerk" and "idiot".

6 Disco Pals

Alecia and Patti are best friends. At the school dance, Alecia makes fun of Patti's dancing, saying white girls can't dance.

9 Racial Profiling

Every time Jamie, who is Middle Eastern, goes into the mall, the security officers follow him around and the cashiers check his packages extra carefully.

7 One World

Frank catches his little brother trying to wash the colour off his friend.

10 Money Matter$

When Chad, who recently transferred from a reserve school, asks his teacher about the class trip, Mr. Harris asks if he can afford it.

8 Being Bullied

The youngest of this group of kids, who are all Jewish, is always getting bullied.

Answers

1. No. Not knowing something or making a mistake isn't racist. But how about taking the opportunity to learn about differences between these ethnicities?

2. This is racism only if Jenny is being excluded because she is Black.

3. No. The Newfoundlander joke was insensitive, but not racist because it's based on a stereotype about a culture, not a race. An explanation of the difference is on page 10.

4. Yes, but only if Lien's teacher meant that he assumed she must be good at math because she is Asian.

5. No. Since the boys don't refer to each other's race, this isn't racism — but it's pretty unfriendly!

6. No. Although the teasing does refer to a racial stereotype, it doesn't put either girl at a disadvantage.

7. No. Frank's little brother is not being unfair to his friend, he's just too young to understand about skin colour.

8. No. Bullying is always unfair, but it's not racism when the bully and target are of the same race.

9. Yes, if Jamie is being treated differently because of his race. Being more likely to commit a crime is one of the stereotypes that people of colour often have to deal with.

10. Yes, if Mr. Harris has assumed Chad is poor because of a racial stereotype.

Racism 101

Dear Conflict Counsellor

Q: I'm really confused. What's the difference between race, ethnicity, and nationality? And how do you know if someone is from a minority group?
— *All mixed up*

A: Basically, a person is from a minority group when they are not considered part of the majority, or most dominant, group. Race is usually defined by skin colour and other physical traits. Ethnicity refers to the region where a person was born. People of the same ethnicity may share cultural traits, such as language and traditions. Nationality is the same as citizenship. It simply refers to the country where you live. Whew, that's a lot to grasp.

more divisions. Don't buy into the stereotypes.

Q: I am the only person of colour in my class. My grades are bad, and I think it may be due to racism. People assume I want to be left alone, so I feel lonely a lot of the time. What should I do?

— *The Loner*

A: You won't know if your troubles are caused by racism until you try to change your situation. Speak with your teachers about your grades — don't just make excuses for your marks. Help the kids get to know you — join clubs and teams and participate in school activities. Ask your teacher or guidance counsellor to help you develop a strategy.

Q: There is a small group of Black kids that hang out together at my school. I hear them calling each other names that are so racist! If a white kid used those words, the group would get really mad. So how come it's okay for them to talk to each other like that?

— *Offended*

A: As part of a minority at your school, these kids need to find their comfort zone within their own group. Sometimes people who have felt the sting of racism will use the language that has hurt them, trying to lessen its power. Does that make it okay for those kids to use words that many people find offensive? Not everyone agrees. But you know that if you used those words, it would cause harm — so don't use them.

Q: Divisions in our school are all about money. People assume that all the Jewish and Asian kids have money and that the Black and Aboriginal kids are poor. Why do we separate people into categories?

— *Haves and Have-nots*

A: Racial stereotypes like these are the result of a lot of misinformation and often fear. If the opinion is positive (like assuming someone does have money), people often don't realize that it can still be harmful. When we assume anything about someone, it only encourages more assumptions and

Q: Lately, I've been hearing a lot about anti-Semitism and Islamophobia. When you attack someone's religion, is it racism?

— *Muddled Up*

A: Not strictly. But religion can be a significant part of a person's racial identity and heritage, so religious conflicts are often part of racial conflicts. 'Anti-Semitism' refers to stereotypes, prejudice, and discrimination against Jewish people, and 'Islamophobia' refers to stereotypes, prejudice, and discrimination against Muslims.

Myths

One person can't change anything.

While racism is a common experience for many people, you must decide if you want to be part of the problem or part of the solution.

Human rights laws have gotten rid of racism.

Laws have reduced racist acts within schools and workplaces, but laws alone cannot change attitudes, and many people still hold racist beliefs.

It's not a STEREOTYPE if it's positive.

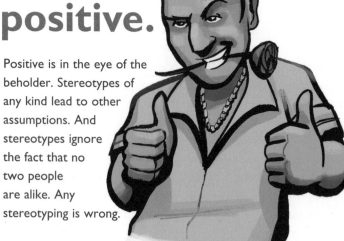

Positive is in the eye of the beholder. Stereotypes of any kind lead to other assumptions. And stereotypes ignore the fact that no two people are alike. Any stereotyping is wrong.

DID YOU KNOW?

- **20%** of visible minorities sometimes or often experience racism.

Immigrants
are taking all the jobs.

Fewer people are entering the work force than are leaving it, so immigration is necessary to have enough workers in North America.

Only **white people** have **racist attitudes.**

Anyone can believe a stereotype about anyone else, or behave in a discriminating way.

- **1/3** of Blacks sometimes or often experience racism.

- **25%** of the population (over age 15) was born outside Canada.

- Canadian schools separated Black and white children in the school system until the second half of the 20th century.

So, you're the outsider.

You feel outnumbered, and are tired of being treated differently. People may not realize when they're being racist, but it still hurts. Sometimes you just wish you could fit in instead of being stuck in the minority.

There's no question it can be tough to be part of the minority. Some people believe that members of minority groups:

• are more likely to be involved in crime
• are more likely to get away with crime
• have no respect
• are dangerous or unpredictable
• are intolerant about other religions
• have poor hygiene
• are not as smart
• are lazy and don't want to work
• threaten to take over from other groups
• are poor
• are taking all the jobs
• have too much power and influence

These are hard attitudes to deal with, but remember that millions of people, of all races, are combating racism around the world. You are not alone.

do's and don'ts

✓ Do speak to your parents or another trustworthy adult.

✓ Do realize that lots of people experience, and overcome, discrimination.

✓ Do educate yourself about the history of racism and its effects.

✓ Do stay with your friends, especially if you feel frightened.

✓ Do open your mind to other friendships.

✓ Do show pride in your uniqueness.

✓ Do try to avoid people who are racist.

✓ Do try to be assertive.

✗ Don't let racism make you hate yourself.

✗ Don't blame yourself for the ignorance of others.

✗ Don't try to solve the problem all by yourself. Get help.

✗ Don't hate back.

✗ Don't become prejudiced about all members of the majority group.

QUIZ

How do you handle racism?

Do you ignore it? Do you speak out? Do you give people a taste of their own medicine? There are three basic ways you can respond to prejudice — acting **powerlessly**, becoming **empowered**, or acting **overpowered**. Responding powerlessly does nothing to stop the hate, and acting overpowered, or aggressively, only promotes hate and intolerance. But if you behave in a way that shows you are empowered, you can fight racism. Take this quiz and then check out your behaviour at the bottom of the page.

1 Holiday Cheerlessness

You don't celebrate Christmas, and in December you feel left out and isolated. Do you: a) Say nothing? b) Knock over the Christmas tree and call the teacher a racist? c) Speak with teachers about celebrating other holidays?

3 WHITE BOYS CAN JUMP

Joey is white, and wants to join the group of mostly Black kids who play basketball at recess, but he feels that maybe they don't want him to play. Should he: a) Leave them alone? b) Call them names, yelling at them for excluding the white kids? c) Get to know the kids and work on developing friendships?

2 TOTALLY UNCOOL

A group of older kids keep pulling off your Hijab, but your parents insist you wear your headdress every day. Next time it happens, do you: a) Punch the ringleader in the stomach? b) Tell the teacher and your parents? c) Hide your Hijab in your backpack before you get to school?

4 INVISIBLE

Jabari is sick of reading books that don't have positive Black characters. The magazines and newspapers at his school are the same. Should he: a) Join a group that raises money to buy culturally diverse books? b) Say nothing? c) Make fun of all the "white trash" characters in the books?

5 ALL ALIKE

The bus driver keeps mistaking Connie for other Asian kids that go to her school. She even got blamed for picking on a younger kid because the driver couldn't tell the difference between her and another girl. Should she: a) Make a joke about her own race to bring it to the driver's attention? b) Keep telling the bus driver her name in a clear, firm voice, and possibly speak with her teacher? c) Take the blame for picking on the kid?

6 GRAFFITI GUILT

The bathroom walls at Joseph's school are covered in racist graffiti. He sees it everyday and, for some reason, he feels guilty. Sometimes he wishes he hadn't immigrated. Should he: a) Move? b) Get help to encourage the school to clean up the graffiti? c) Write nasty things on top of the graffiti?

7 SAVAGE STEREOTYPES

The school sports mascot is a stereotypical Native "savage." Catherine, who is Métis, feels angry every time the mascot prances around pretending to "scalp" people. Should she:
a) Throw candy wrappers at him? b) Laugh at the silly tradition.
c) Bring information to the school administration about the history of Aboriginal people and ask them to hold a contest to come up with a new team mascot?

8 HOTDOG HOLDOUT

Every Friday, the school sells hotdogs to raise money for the class trip. T. J.'s religion does not allow him to eat pork. Should he: a) Ask the teachers if they could order vegetarian wieners? b) Make a huge big stink about it? c) Just don't eat the hotdogs?

Answers

1. a) powerless b) overpowered c) empowered	4. a) empowered b) powerless c) overpowered	7. a) overpowered b) powerless c) empowered
2. a) overpowered b) empowered c) powerless	5. a) overpowered b) empowered c) powerless	8. a) empowered b) overpowered c) powerless
3. a) powerless b) overpowered c) empowered	6. a) powerless b) empowered c) overpowered	9. a) empowered b) powerless c) overpowered

10. a) overpowered b) powerless c) empowered

9 The Right to Wear

Fadi wears a turban, but his camp counsellor refuses to allow him to wear it during athletic activities. Should he:
a) Ask his parents to bring it to the camp administrator's attention.
b) Just stop wearing the turban? c) Steal the camp counsellor's hat and see how he likes it?

10 Suspicious Minds

A group of Black kids feel targeted by school security. They all agree that they get suspicious looks, and their lockers get checked more often. Should they:
a) Walk right up a security officer and ask him what his problem is? b) Just ignore the suspicious looks? c) Join or start up a peer empowerment group to work on anti-racism education?

There are some basic things you can do
to protect yourself against racism.

Explore Your Feelings

Racism is often subtle and hard to define. Listen to what your gut is telling you. If you feel like an outsider, try to figure out why. Try to identify the attitudes and behaviours that have made you feel separate. Counselling often helps to sort out feelings of anger, isolation, fear, and sadness.

Speak Up

If you experience discrimination in any form, speak up. This strategy works best if you have friends around you. Never try this if you believe you are in physical danger. If your tormentors refuse to change, tell a trusted adult. Report hate crimes to the police.

Be Proactive

Join clubs or groups where you feel welcomed. Peer groups will help you feel less alone. There is strength in numbers to educate people about racism and its effects, and to promote understanding of the cultures and customs of ethnic groups.

Explore Your History

To protect yourself against the effects of prejudice, it is important that you know your own background. Speak to your family members, read books, and contact groups in your community. Be proud of your roots.

DID YOU KNOW ?

- To get rid of racism, we must consider all the different types of discrimination.

- Right up to the 1970s, thousands of Aboriginal children were sent to

When the System Is Involved

Often racism is rooted within "systems," such as education system (schools) or the justice system (policing and courts). This is called systemic racism, and it leads to unfairness toward minority people.

One example is when members of minority groups are given fewer opportunities at school or work because the people in power believe they are not as qualified. This kind of excluding might not be intentional, but it is still very harmful.

Racial profiling is another type of systemic racism. If police believe the myth that members of minority groups commit more crimes, people of colour will be suspected more often.

In schools, the administration may purchase books that don't show experiences of minority groups — which can make some students feel excluded.

And if employers or landlords assume new immigrants and people of colour won't work hard to pay their bills, they may turn away members of minority groups.

Systemic racism is a difficult challenge to overcome because it doesn't focus on one person's behaviour or attitude. Because it's a whole system someone is up against, it may seem impossible to overcome. It can lead to blaming everyone in the majority — so the hate just gets bigger and bigger. That's why everyone must take responsibility for breaking down barriers and defeating racism.

Educate Yourself
Racism is deeply rooted in our history. Though we have come a very long way, we still have a long way to go before we can put an end to racism. And knowledge is a powerful weapon against hate.

residential schools, where they were punished for trying to maintain their culture.

- Incidents of anti-Semitism more than doubled from 2001 to 2003.

- Genocide or ethnic cleansing is the use of violence to wipe out an entire race or culture.

- Racism can make people feel depressed, scared, isolated, and sad.

Hey, you're not racist, are you?

No way. Those skinheads who attack minorities and spray-paint graffiti on walls, they're racist. That's not you. Maybe sometimes you feel like all the minority groups are taking over the school. And maybe you do a few killer impersonations of certain racial groups. And, okay, maybe you feel really weird and nervous going into neighborhoods where you're so obviously not in the majority.

But <u>you're</u> not racist. Are you?

DEAR DR. SHRINK-WRAPPED...

Q: This new kid at school wears a turban. So of course, we kept trying to grab at it during recess. It was just teasing, but now the whole class has to study Sikh culture and traditions. Weren't they the terrorists responsible for September 11, 2001?

— *Just Teasing*

A: Many people all over the world have been fearful since the tragic events of September 11, 2001. The increased need for security has been used to justify stereotyping and blaming all people of Middle Eastern descent. Your teacher is helping you understand the many reasons people are afraid or intolerant of differences. For example:

- Things we don't understand can make us uncomfortable.
- We may have heard our parents or friends make unkind remarks about minorities.
- We see stereotypical images of people on television and the Internet (for example, people of colour repeatedly featured only as athletes, musicians, or gangsters).
- The books we read and movies we watch have mostly white characters, especially the heroes.
- The music we listen to may have racist language.
- We are afraid of not fitting in and fear the unknown.
- We might not understand the privileges and advantages we have, or we don't want to lose them.
- We don't realize the harm done by our attitudes and behaviour.

In difficult times, it's easy to hate whole nations of people for the actions of individuals — but it's just plain wrong.

Q: My friends don't know that my dad is from Jamaica because my skin is very light. I laugh at the jokes my friends tell about Black people; I've even told a few. What harm can come of avoiding racism this way?

— *Inconspicuous*

A: Dr. Shrink-Wrapped thinks you are afraid of being rejected and are trying to pretend racism doesn't hurt you or anyone. But silence can build a wall of shame around you, and now you are part of the problem. It may be hard for you, but it is important for you to come clean with your friends because:

- You may start to believe the negative stereotypes about your race.
- Your fear of becoming an outsider is unfair to other people in the minority.
- Hating who you are may cause depression and low self-esteem.
- Kids who feel excluded sometimes join gangs to feel like they belong.
- Feeling hated may cause you to lash out at others.
- Intolerant attitudes turn into racist behaviours like discrimination.
- Your silence says racism is okay.

QUIZ

Personal differences or racism?

Remind you of anyone? Answer the following true or false questions to find out where you weigh in on the competition scale.

1. I have been accused of racism.

2. I am impatient with people who are different.

3. I tend to blame others for the problems in the world.

4. I have laughed at racist jokes.

5. There are particular people I don't like to be around.

6. Some people don't deserve respect.

7. I think people of colour aren't as smart as white people.

8. I have told jokes about people wearing turbans or veils.

9. People have told me I am not very open-minded.

10. I think it's none of my business when I see people getting hurt.

11. I say racist things when I'm angry.

12. Some cultural stereotypes are true.

13. I don't like being different.

I think there's nothing I can do about racism. **14**

I am shy around new people. **15**

I don't question what I see or read in the media. **16**

Change is hard for me. **17**

Admitting mistakes is even harder for me. **18**

My family doesn't like minorities. **19**

My friends are all the same as me. **20**

I think people from minority groups are responsible for most crime. **21**

Minority groups are basically lazy and unwilling to help themselves. **22**

I've been called a bully. **23**

There are too many immigrants. **24**

Positive stereotypes are no big deal. **25**

People's accents annoy me. **26**

People should stick to their own kind. **27**

Racism really isn't a problem today. **28**

I feel like white people are discriminated against. **29**

I wish some people would go back to where they came from. **30**

Did you score a lot of Trues? Maybe you should talk to someone about why you generalize about people rather than getting to know them.

How can you stop racism?

There are many things you can do to stop being part of the problem of racism:

Examine your own behaviour and attitudes toward people who are different from you. Open your mind and heart. It takes a lot of guts to admit you made a mistake. If possible, apologize to any people you have hurt.

Learn about the history of racism in this country and around the world. Research the struggles of Aboriginal people, enslaved Africans, and Chinese immigrants during Canada's developing years. Learn about the history behind military conflicts around the world. Bring in speakers from local groups to help you appreciate the difficulties new immigrants face.

Question the images you see in the media. People from minority groups are often portrayed in certain ways in TV shows, films, videos, and books. Learn to look for the misinformation behind stereotypes. Organize a school dance to raise funds to purchase books, posters, artwork, and videos that more accurately reflect your school's diversity.

Clean up racist graffiti at your school and in the neighbourhood. Encourage your school to develop its own anti-racism policies. Get involved.

Form a Culture Club at your school to promote harmony and respect. Familiarize yourself with the customs and cultures of other groups. Plan awareness events for March 21, the International Day for the Elimination of Racial Discrimination.

Challenge your friends. Speak to them about the things you've learned. If you and your friends are accustomed to making racist jokes, be prepared — they may not want to change. But keep trying.

DID YOU KNOW?

- Some people feel so beaten down by racism that it causes significant underachievement and low self-esteem.

Nobody said it would be easy to become more tolerant! It's okay to feel uncomfortable, shy, or unsure of yourself. Remember, racism is something you have learned; no one was ever born a racist. Unlearning prejudice can be difficult, especially if you are surrounded by people who are intolerant of cultural differences. But keep trying, and soon you will be part of the solution, instead of part of the problem.

do's and don'ts

✓ Do educate yourself.

✓ Do think about your language before you speak or write.

✓ Do look for ways to challenge racism.

✓ Do speak out if you see hate-motivated acts.

✓ Do embrace the idea of "one-world."

✓ Do reach out when you see someone hurt by racism.

✓ Do work on your comfort level with new people.

✓ Do apologize to people you have hurt.

✓ Do think about the consequences of racist acts.

✗ Don't be closed-minded.

✗ Don't be disrespectful.

✗ Don't be afraid of differences.

✗ Don't let your shyness stop you.

✗ Don't give up.

✗ Don't retaliate if someone resents you as part of the dominant group.

- Xenophobia is when the dominant group fears "foreigners" or "outsiders."

- Many people within minority groups — Jews, Muslims, Sikhs, Aboriginals, Hindus, Asians, Blacks — are targets of hate crimes.

Have you ever been around when someone told a racist joke?

Did you tell the joker that you didn't think it was funny?

No?

Well, what stopped you?

People Power

Often people don't recognize subtle forms of prejudice. They may not understand that their silence sends the message that racism is okay. By speaking up or taking a stand, witnesses may fear they will:

- lose friends
- interfere in something that's none of their business
- be accused of being overly sensitive
- get someone in trouble

Sometimes witnesses think that racism is too big a challenge, and that one person can't create change. But you have the power to make a difference!

do's and don'ts

✓ Do educate yourself about racism.

✓ Do learn about other cultures and customs.

✓ Do treat everyone with respect.

✓ Do tell a trustworthy adult when you see culture clash happening.

✓ Do get help — a teacher, supervisor, principal, neighbour, parent, or older friend.

✓ Do set a good example for others.

✓ Do speak up. Get involved.

✓ Do offer assistance and friendship to the target.

✗ Don't copy the discrimination.

✗ Don't seek revenge for racist acts.

✗ Don't encourage the attacker by laughing.

✗ Don't stand by and do nothing.

✗ Don't give up trying. Change happens one person at a time.

The **Witness**

QUIZ

Do you really get it?

So you think the next time you witness racism, you'll recognize it and know what to do. But do you really get it? What would you do in the following situations? This quiz doesn't really have any right or wrong answers because each example of racism is unique. Your answers may be different from the suggestions offered, but they could also be right under the circumstances.

① NOT FUNNY

You hear your friends making racist jokes. No one else is around so nobody gets hurt. Right?

- Tell jokes that do not target minority groups.
- Walk away if they persist.
- Speak up. Tell your friends that you don't think the jokes are funny.
- **Wrong.** Racist jokes lead to stereotypes and discrimination, or treating people unfairly.

② SIT TIGHT

No one will sit near the new kid on the bus. You can tell he feels pretty isolated and sad. He has trouble speaking English, so you haven't really spoken with him before. What should you do?

- Invite him to join some activities at school.
- Use books, pictures, or music to help communicate with each other.
- Try to make small talk. You might be surprised by how much he understands the language.
- A good place to start is in the seat next to him on the bus.

③ Take a Dance Chance

You think the new girl from Sierra Leone is gorgeous, but you're afraid that if you ask her to the dance, you'll make a really odd couple. Is it worth all the stress?

- Yes it is. Start by de-stressing the situation by becoming friends with the girl.
- Talk to your friends. You might be surprised by their attitude.
- Ask her to the dance, and tell your friends not to be jealous that you'll have the prettiest date there.

④ Singing the Blues

Your school has a new policy that no "gangster" music is allowed at dances. You know that means no hip-hop — your favourite — and now no one wants to go to the dance. Is there anything you can do?

- Ask the school administration for an explanation of the policy. It likely has to do with the lyrics.
- Assure the administration that students can help them choose songs that are not offensive. Get your parents' help, if necessary.
- Ask the administration for a chance to prove that, whatever music is being played, students can behave well at the dance. And then make sure that everyone does!

⑤ The Colour of Friendship

Sam used to be your best friend, but you don't hang out with him any longer because his family doesn't trust you. They thought that, because you are Black, you must be in a gang. They were always giving you a hard time.

- Understand that interracial friendships can have their challenges. Decide if intolerance is worth losing a friend over.
- Call your friend! Talk through your feelings and concerns.
- Help your friend's family get to know you, to help build their trust.
- Let your friend's family meet your family, so they can see that there is not so much difference between you.

Continues . . .

29

⑥ HATE CRIME

Someone has spray-painted swastikas all over the windows of the local Hebrew day school. You overheard some kids on your baseball team laughing about it, and they named the guys who did it. What do you do?

- All vandalism is destructive. But racist vandalism strikes fear into entire communities. It is your responsibility to take a stand against hate.
- Because it is a criminal act, it is best not to speak to the kids involved. Seek the help of your parents or teachers.
- With the support of a trusted adult, speak to the police.
- Find out how you, your friends, and your school can help clean up the graffiti and

⑧ *Bullying on the Bus*

The new kid on the bus is from Pakistan and the class bully roughs him up all the time. You know it isn't right, but you don't want to be the bully's next target. What do you do?

- Offer to sit with the new kid on the bus. Give him your support.
- Encourage him to speak with his parents and teacher.
- Tell the bus driver and report the incident to your teacher at school.
- There is strength in numbers — if all the kids support the new kid, the bus bully can't get away with terrorizing everyone.

⑦ **Southern Exposure**

Marco is originally from South America. Sometimes the kids call him Mexican and other times Spanish.

- There are significant differences between these cultures, and there's no excuse for remaining ignorant about them.
- Show Marco you care and ask him about his birthplace — get to know him.
- When someone mistakenly identifies Marco's background, casually set them straight.

⑨ *Bad Babysitter*

Your friend's little sister confided in you that her babysitter teases her by calling her names that are pretty racist. She doesn't want to tell her parents, but she is getting more and more upset. What can you do?

- Tell her that you're glad she said something and that you're sorry she's being treated that way.
- Talk to her about why she doesn't want to tell her parents. She may be reluctant to get her babysitter fired, especially if she likes her. There may be another solution.
- Offer to go with her for support when she tells her parents or another family member.

⑩ IT'S EVERYONE'S PROBLEM

No one in your class is openly racist. But sometimes you have felt they weren't really getting it when racism was being discussed. And most of the kids don't see why racism should matter to them. What more can be done?

- Ask your teacher if the class can invite guests to come speak on racism and human rights and show films about stereotyping, discrimination, and diversity.
- Initiate a class discussion on the stereotypes in television, films, music videos, and newspapers.
- Suggest the class does research on individual family trees to learn about everyone's different backgrounds and histories.

- Surveys show that more than half of Canadians admit to being "somewhat" racist
- March 21 is the International Day for the Elimination of Racial Discrimination
- There is power in diversity

More Help

It takes time and practice to learn the skills in this book. There are many ways to deal with racism but only you can know which feels right in each situation. In the end, the best response is the one that prevents everyone from being hurt or treated unfairly.

If you need more information, or someone to talk to, the following resources may be of help.

Helplines and Organizations

Kids Help Phone: 1-800-668-6868
Justice for Children and Youth: 1-866-999-JFCY
Canadian Race Relations Foundation: 1-888-240-4936
Anti-Hate Hotline: 1-800-892-2624

Web sites

Canadian Safe Schools Network: www.cssn.org
Kids Help Phone: www.kidshelp.sympatico.ca
Canadian Race Relations Foundation: www.crr.ca
Anti-racism educational site: www.tolerance.org
Equality Today: www.equalitytoday.org
Racism. Stop it!: www.pch.gc.ca/march-21-mars/main_e.shtml
Youth Forums Against Racism: www.unac.org

Books

A Group of One by Rachna Gilmore, Henry Holt & Co. Ltd., 2001.
Across the Steel River by Ted Stenhouse, Kids Can Press, 2001.
Angel Square by Brian Doyle. Groundwood Books, 1984.
As Long as the Rivers Flow by Oskiniko Larry Loyie and Constance Brissenden. Groundwood Books, 2003.
Breakaway by Paul Yee. Groundwood Books, 1994.
Emily: Building Bridges by Julie Lawson. Penguin Canada, 2003.
Hana's Suitcase: A True Story by Karen Levine. Second Story Press, 2002.
I Came as a Stranger: The Underground Railroad by Bryan Prince. Tundra Books, 2004.
Rachel: The Maybe House by Lynne Kositsky. Penguin Canada, 2002.
Taking Sides by Sylvia Gunneray, Scholastic, 1991.
The Liberty Circle by Phil Campagna, Napoleon, 2000.
Wrong Time, Wrong Place by Lesley Choyce. Formac Publishing, 1991.
Zack by William Bell. Doubleday Canada, 1998.

Videos

Playing Fair: Anti-racism series. National Film Board of Canada, 1992. (www.nfb.ca, 1-800-267-7710)
Nobody's Born a Racist. The Students Commission, 1996.
For Angela. National Film Board of Canada, 1995.
Taking charge. National Film Board of Canada, 1996.

Manufactured by Paramount Printing Company Limited in Tseung Kwan O, New Territories, Hong Kong in 2010.
Job Number: 130745

James Lorimer & Company Ltd. acknowledges the support of the Ontario Arts Council. We acknowledge the financial support of the Government of Canada through the Canada Book Fund for our publishing activities. We acknowledge the support of the Canada Council for the Arts for our publishing program. We acknowledge the support of the Government of Ontario through the Ontario Media Development Corporation's Ontario Book Initiative.

First published in the United States in 2011.

The Canada Council | Le Conseil des Arts
for the Arts | du Canada

ONTARIO ARTS COUNCIL
CONSEIL DES ARTS DE L'ONTARIO

Design: Blair Kerrigan/Glyphics

Library and Archives Canada Cataloguing in Publication

Aikins, Anne Marie
    Racism : deal with it before it gets under your skin / Anne Marie Aikins ; illustrated by Steven Murray.

(Deal with it)
ISBN 978-1-55277-495-3 (bound)
ISBN 978-1-55028-844-5 (pbk.)

    1. Racism—Juvenile literature. I. Murray, Steven II. Title.
III. Series: Deal with it (Toronto, Ont.)

BF723.P75A34 2010   j305.8   C2010-900276-8

James Lorimer & Company Ltd., Publishers
317 Adelaide Street West, Suite #1002
Toronto, Ontario
M5V 1P9
www.lorimer.ca

Distributed in the United States by:
Orca Book Publishers
P.O. Box 468
Custer, WA USA
98240-0468

Printed and bound in Hong Kong